The Great Book of Dragons

Text by Federica Magrin

Illustrations by Anna Láng

WSkids
WHITE STAR KIDS

Contents

Introduction

Hi! If you picked this book, it means you're just like me, a curious kid who's crazy about dragons.

My interest in them came about by chance. I was out walking in the woods one day when I came across a strange round object. It looked like an egg but it was much bigger than a normal one. It was a dragon's egg, that's why, a Wyvern to be precise. I found that out when I left the egg under an infrared lamp for a while and a strange little snout poked out, a bit like a crocodile's but different.

Living with a baby dragon wasn't easy to begin with, I can tell you! I couldn't control him, he kept puffing smoke out everywhere and getting into trouble. Things improved a bit when I spoke to a dragonologist who explained how to treat him, look after him, and train him.

Everything's fine now. Me and Claw (that's what I called him, do you like it?) are best friends. That's why I decided to write down some tips for future dragon masters. Nothing complicated or serious. But since there are also dragons who can't be tamed and some that are downright dangerous, I've also added some tips on how to defeat a dragon. Just in case, you never know when you might need it!

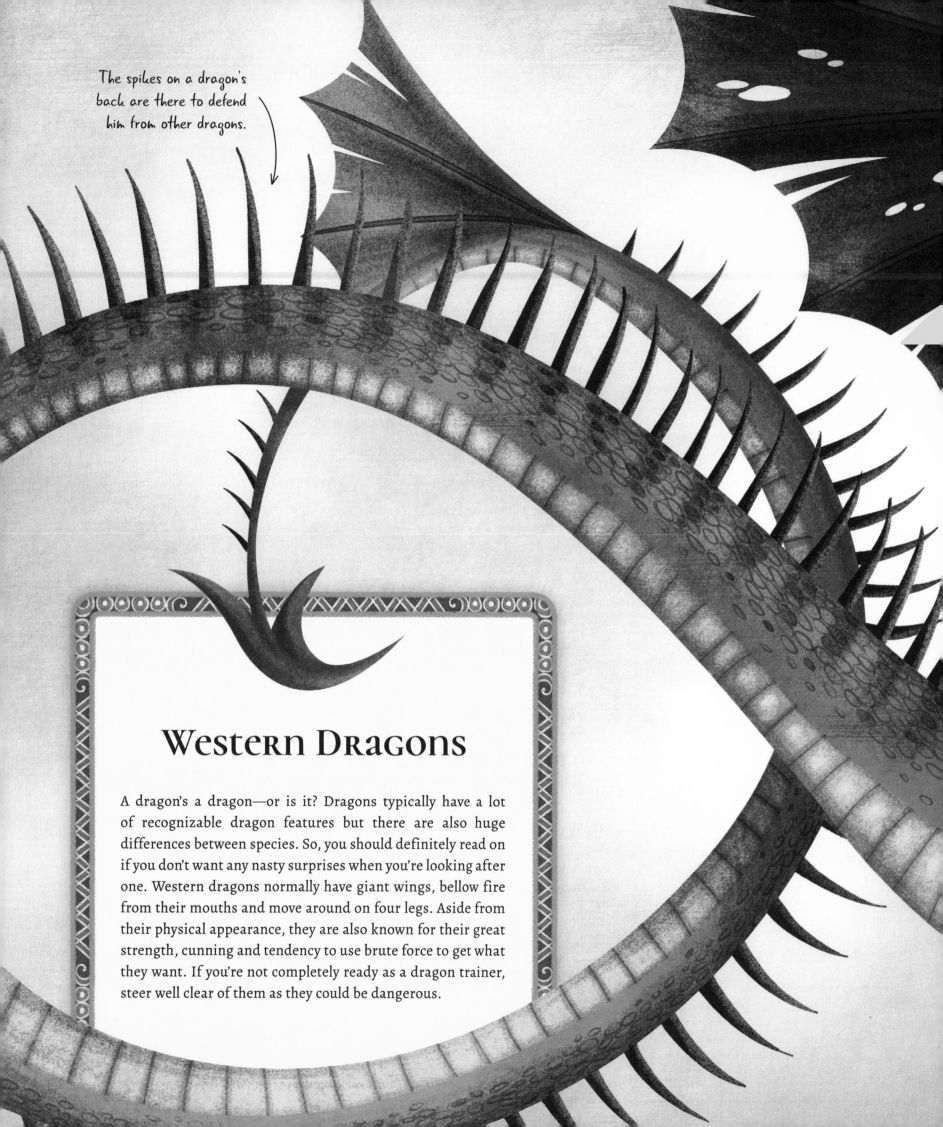

The spikes on a dragon's back are there to defend him from other dragons.

Western Dragons

A dragon's a dragon—or is it? Dragons typically have a lot of recognizable dragon features but there are also huge differences between species. So, you should definitely read on if you don't want any nasty surprises when you're looking after one. Western dragons normally have giant wings, bellow fire from their mouths and move around on four legs. Aside from their physical appearance, they are also known for their great strength, cunning and tendency to use brute force to get what they want. If you're not completely ready as a dragon trainer, steer well clear of them as they could be dangerous.

The wings are similar to a bat's and can withstand very high temperatures.

The flames spewed from the dragon's mouth can reach ten feet or more.

The claws on its feet are to grasp prey and dig tunnels in the ground.

Knucker

If I had to describe the Knucker dragon in a word, that word would be … terrible! Knucker is one of the most ferocious water dragons to exist, capable of destroying whole villages by devouring everything around its lair, which is a seemingly bottomless water-hole. Knuckers stay underwater most of the time although some have wings and are able to fly. Legend has it that one such dragon was defeated by a boy like you, Jim Pulk he was called. He lay a tempting trap, namely a poisoned cake that the terrifying beast swallowed in a single gulp… along with the horse and cart Jim had used to take the cake to the dragon's den. Before you try the same thing, though, remember that we'll never know if it was the poison that got the gluttonous beast — or indigestion!

The body has a streamlined shape enabling the dragon to slip more easily through the water and swim like a fish.

Watch out for its coils! You could choke in them if a Knucker wrapped them around you like a snake.

A Catalan farmer who saw one once said, "I swear, the smoke bellowing from its mouth would corrode even the toughest of metals!"

How can you tell male and female dragons apart? Often from their coloration, which is brighter on males and more subdued on females. But this is not a hard and fast rule: in the dragon-sphere, you never really know for sure.

Drac

Don't be fooled by the fact it has fewer limbs — only two — because this Catalan dragon can crush any of its fellow dragons, both land and sea, with strength and cunning alone. It's most fabled trait is the ability to kill with its breath, which not only produces terrifying flames but also contains toxic substances that will corrode anything they touch. And don't be tempted to think the she-dragon is any less cruel than the male. Quite the opposite! The *vibria*, as the Catalans call her, is so treacherous, just to look at her is life-threatening!

Just two legs, as I mentioned, but both muscular and strong enough to snatch prey and squeeze it tight in a vice-like grip.

The tail winds itself around the victim, squeezing tight. The sting does the rest, striking the unfortunate captive at blistering speed!

Wyvern

Similar to the Drac, the Wyvern has two legs and a barbed tail used to strike its opponents. But that's not all! According to legend, it also has feline traits — the way it hunts, the same cunning when it meets other creatures, and excellent night vision. Humans have always been so fascinated by this legendary beast, which some describe as green and others brown, that it has often ended up in the heraldry of nobles and knights, like the kingdom of Wessex flag, for example. The most famous Wyvern dragon, Thyrus, was slain in the Middle Ages by a young and brave knight who went into the swamp where the treacherous reptile lived.

A dragon's skin, either green or brown, helps it to blend in with its surroundings and ambush its prey in murderous surprise attacks.

The long body has to be wound into spirals to take up as little space as possible.

The blood of some dragons, Fafnir's for example, can make the human body indestructible.

Lindworm

Lindworm describes a series of dragons who differ quite significantly from each other but have a serpentine body shape in common. Being snake-like, they can slither furtively through the forest without being seen, a fatal skill for anyone not expecting a dragon to appear before them! Famous Lindworms include the dragon of Yggdrasil, a mythical tree in Norse mythology; the Midgard Serpent, an implacable enemy of thunder-god Thor that grew so long it could surround the earth; and the mighty Fafnir, a dwarf turned dragon that was defeated by the legendary hero Sigurd.

This dragon's mantle is red like fire but takes on copper hues in the sun that give off real sparks.

Y Ddraig Goch

The Y Ddraig Goch has links to Merlin the wizard. When the powerful enchanter was just a boy, he informed King Vortigern that there were two monstrous creatures in the ground under his castle, one white and one red, and their violent clashes were causing the castle's foundations and walls to continuously collapse. The destructive red dragon was Y Ddraig Goch, the famous monster of formidable power.

Not one but three, or seven or even nine heads all with wide-open mouths baring scythe-like teeth.

Zmaj

Dragons with one head are scary enough, imagine seeing a Zmaj with not two but anything from three up to nine heads! One such creature, which looks like a snake but has clawed feet and huge wings on its gigantic body, was apparently defeated at the beginning of time by Svarog, the God of Fire, who used Zmaj like an enormous plough to make the earth fertile.

Zomok

Zomok looks like a dragon but is actually a nature spirit whose main purpose is to protect plant and animal life. It scours the forests to check for wildfires and make sure no trees are being chopped down, and is also able to cure, restore or reform anything damaged by man or other creatures. Despite being a positive figure that is very useful to the earth, Zomok is also dangerous, showing its enemies or anyone harming the planet no mercy.

Rocks, branches, dust and leaves all blast out of its enormous jaws, slamming brutally into its foes.

It constantly shapeshifts to blend in and better mimic the colors of the natural world around it.

Zomok's body is comprised of vegetable parts, enabling it to blend in perfectly with the thick growth of the forest.

A special substance flows in its blood,
stopping it from freezing, even at
-130 °F (-90 °C).

Ice Dragons

The ice dragon is one of the most fascinating and
mysterious creatures of its kind. It is a rare species, with
only very few remaining, and it tends to stay away from
humans. The name comes from the color of its scales,
which vary from white to light blue, like the ice covering
its natural habitat. It doesn't like the heat but if need be,
when it moves from one pole to the other for instance, it can
survive high temperatures. When the opportunity arises,
though, it will dive straight into the icy polar waters to cool
down. Don't be fooled by the noble, elegant way it moves.
It's no less treacherous than other dragons. In fact, the
glacial jet shooting from its mouth could kill a much bigger
animal on the spot.

If you take a closer look at the scales,
you'll see other colors, not just white
and blue, but all just as cold!

The ridges and spikes on its body help
the dragon blend into the ice pack.

Pads under its feet keep it from slipping
when it walks on ice.

The long whiskers give the eastern dragon a comical look but don't let this fool you: it's anything but a circus animal.

Eastern Dragons

The eastern dragon has the same essential features as its western counterpart but differs in that it is normally wingless, has a long serpentine body and often has ornamental feathers on various parts of its body.

Supremely astute and having great wisdom, the eastern dragon is more likely to bond with humans. But don't think you can keep one as a pet, it may take offence and try to avenge itself. If you do all the right things, though, and manage to make friends, it could bring you a lot of good luck. This is one kind of dragon it might be worthwhile looking after.

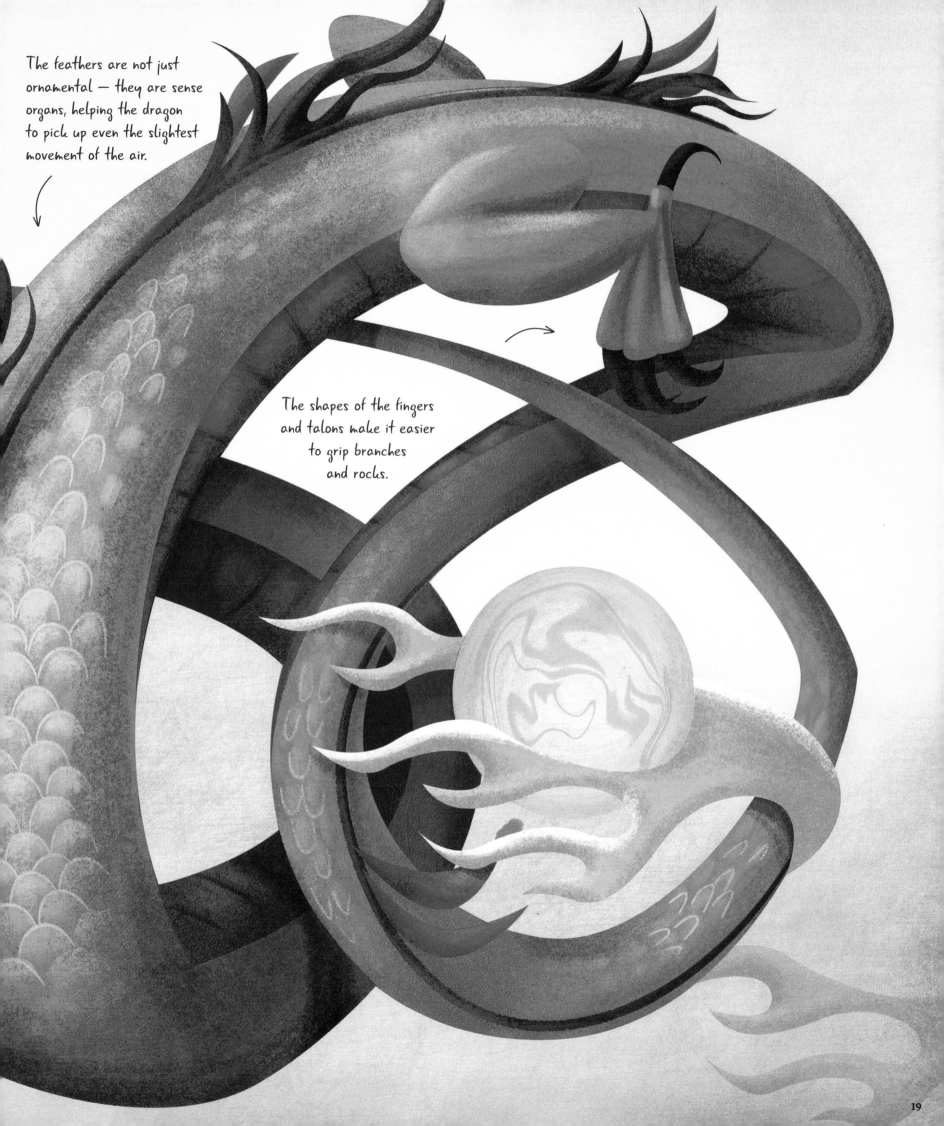

The feathers are not just ornamental — they are sense organs, helping the dragon to pick up even the slightest movement of the air.

The shapes of the fingers and talons make it easier to grip branches and rocks.

Lung

The Lung is the most representative of the eastern dragons, being typically wingless with a long, serpentine body, head like a large crocodile and catfish-like whiskers hanging from its mouth. Other distinctive features include horns like a deer only shorter, and a much greater bulk than other dragons in Asia. The Lung is also the archetypal benevolent dragon, a bringer of good fortune and prosperity to receptive souls crossing its path. Its natural habitat is in water and many believe this dragon is responsible for the rains that sustain the earth and form rivers, lakes and seas. To meet one and become its friend is a promise of great things.

Despite is size, the Lung is extremely agile and runs so fast it whips up real whirlwinds as it passes.

Lung dragons have many colors although the most typical, especially in noble kinds, are red and gold.

The whiskers are not purely aesthetic, as they are for human men. They are a sense organ. It is said that the Lung sees more with its whiskers than with its eyes!

Dragons are so important in Chinese culture that a great festival has been dedicated to them.

Naga

Naga dragons are a little unusual as they are half-human, half-serpent. Their physical appearance is not the only thing that's different: they are associated with being the guardians of nature, bodies of water in particular, so ponds, lakes, rivers... Another incredible trait that Naga dragons have is immortality. It is said that some tried to steal the nectar of eternal life from the gods but were discovered. A little of the nectar spilled out onto the ground and the dragons leapt to lick it up, acquiring eternal life but paying for it with their tongues which were split in two forever.

In some legends, Nagas live in the underworld while other traditions describe underwater cities populated by these dragons.

Naga dragons have forked tongues like snakes, forever split in two by the magical nectar of eternal life.

Some Naga dragons have multiple heads.

Nagas can bring rains to irrigate fields, or storms to destroy them.

DRUK

A positive creature able to bridge heaven and earth, this dragon lives in the Himalayas and is known as Druk. It is often associated with wealth and prosperity, regularly depicted lying peacefully beside jewels and precious stones. Don't be fooled into thinking it's a friendly animal, though. Druks are powerful and wise but also capable of swiftly taking flight and disappearing into the clouds over the world's highest mountains to defend the men living in this region from evil beings.

One version of the Druk, called "Zeepata", has the body of a dragon and head of a pig.

Druks are also known as "Thunder Dragons" because of their ear-piercing roar.

The treasure they are depicted with symbolizes spiritual, not earthly riches.

This dragon is very sensitive to noise. Its ears can pick up even the quietest whisper which is why the sound of pots and pans were enough to defeat it!

Imagine how big Bakunawa's mouth is if it can eat the moon in a single gulp.

Bakunawa

A dragon of unparalleled terror, this Philippine creature, also known as Bakaunawa meaning "bent snake", is capable of causing terrible catastrophes, like ripping up the earth in surprise earthquakes or submerging everything in water with massive floods. Its most famous trait is the ability to swallow the moon, thrusting the world into darkness. To prevent this, local Filipinos would arm themselves with pots and pans when they saw the dragon arrive and would bang them together with such a deafening racket the dragon would instantly retreat.

Imoogi

The most prominent physical trait of the Korean dragon is its long beard.

A wise, friendly creature, it loves being with humans and will grant almost every favor, no matter how big or small. It is said that meeting an Imugi dragon brings good fortune and can turn even the worst luck around. Four-toed Imugis (one toe serving as a thumb) hold a Yeouiju in their claws. This blue, orb-like globe is extremely valuable and can make wishes come true. Having a Korean dragon as a friend is definitely something to be proud of!

Some Korean dragons have four toes to grip things better.

There are also lesser forms of Korean dragons that are unable to fly but can be blessed with the ability if they catch a Yeouiju.

Neak

Also known as the Khmer dragon, the Neak lives in lesser populated areas of Cambodia. Similar to other Eastern dragons, it is serpent-like and the number of heads it has depends on its rank. If you see one, you'll know how powerful it is at first glance. The highest-ranking ones have nine heads. The Neak only uses its power to do good. It is not a destructive or vindictive dragon, symbolizing only purity of spirit and virtue.

If need be, the Neak can assume human form.

Despite its serpentine appearance, the Khmer dragon possesses a number of crocodilian traits, such as a wide body with short legs on either side.

Ryu

The main characteristics of a Japanese Ryu dragon is that it is wingless, has a long, aerodynamic body and long claws. It often holds a sphere, either a pearl or gemstone, in its feet. In truth, it's actually the Ryu's soul. There are many different kinds of Japanese dragon, able to shapeshift to human form. Generally-speaking, they are all fairly violent and it's not a good idea to get too close.

The appearance of a Ryu is often associated with natural disasters, like torrential rains causing devastating floods.

The fire this dragon produces can move water.

Con Rong

There are 100 Con Rongs. Half of them like to spend their time in their mother's underwater realm and the other half on dry land.

The Vietnamese Con Rong is a special creature. It descends from the union of a dragon and a water fairy. This explains why the Con Rong is a master of both land and water and has characteristics that enable it to live in either environment, like sturdy feet for walking and a streamlined body to slip swiftly through the ocean's waves.

Special Dragons

Some dragons are neither western nor eastern. They have characteristics which are typical of both types and also others which are unique, meaning they could be considered a species of their own. They are strange and sometimes don't even look like dragons, having more in common with animals you see more often, like kangaroos or cockerels. Their behavior is also nothing like "ordinary" dragons, although you should be just as scared — they are powerful, clever and… potentially very dangerous!

Unlike whales with their baleen plates, the Jaffa Dragon has the teeth of a ferocious predator.

Its body shape is ideal for slipping smoothly through the waves.

Jaffa Dragon

In some respects, the sea creature known as the "Dragon of Jaffa" looks like an enormous, serpentine whale with a gigantic crest on its back.

Legend has it that this ravenous, monstrous beast used to roam the eastern shores of the Mediterranean looking for vessels to destroy and humans to devour. Sacrificial victims were often offered in an attempt to placate it. One such time, the Greek hero Perseus stepped in and slayed the dragon to save Andromeda.

MUSHUSSU

Also known as "Sirrush", the Mushussu is a very unusual dragon. Some of its features are closer to those of a "typical dragon", like the serpentine head and scaly body, while others, such as the forelegs of a lion and hind legs of an eagle, give it a rather strange appearance. Unsurprisingly, such an odd-looking creature also has exceptional powers: the strength and agility of a feline, the vision of a bird of prey, and the strike of a snake. These powers of attack and the protective scaly shell make it an invincible war machine.

Sprouting here and there between the scales are tufts of hair. Could this mean that, at some time in the past, it had not only the feet of a lion but also the mane?

At the top of its long neck is a snake's head, and on top of that a large pair of horns.

Tarasca

This monstrous creature, which has several archetypal dragon features, inhabits the southern regions of France, where it spreads death and destruction. Strangely, legend says it can be neutralized through prayer which renders it docile enough to be easily slain. Its appearance is terrifying nevertheless: an enormous body covered with a mantle of scales and spines, a tail it uses like a whip, brawny legs and a ferocious lion's muzzle. The minute you spot one you'll want to get away as fast as you can!

It roars like a lion but highly toxic substances also shoot out from its mouth.

Even though the Tarasca's shell might make it look like a turtle, it is definitely not as peaceful.

Mexican Amphithere

The amphithere dragon loves the warm, humid states of central America, Mexico in particular, where it slithers along the ground like a snake, given that it has no legs. If need be, it can open two large and powerful feathered wings and take to the skies to spot its prey much more easily. Its extra-sharp vision, extra-long tongue and poisonous breath make it a truly frightening creature. Local people are so scared of it, they have built temples and statues in its honor and made abundant offerings of food to stop it from attacking them.

This dragon has many traits in common with the Phoenix, the mythological creature that rose from its ashes.

The amphithere is closely related to the Quetzalcoatl, the plumed serpent that was once worshipped by the Aztecs.

The amphithere's body is covered in both scales and feathers.

Cockatrice

If there is such a thing as a dragon that doesn't look like a dragon, then that's what a Cockatrice is. Its most striking feature is the odd-looking rooster's head, even though the rest of its body is very much that of a two-legged dragon with a thick mantle of scales, a long lizard-like tail and a forked tongue. It is said the cockatrice's strange appearance stems from its unusual origins. Legend has it that it was born from an egg laid by a chicken and incubated for many years by a snake. What makes this creature truly terrifying is its ability to turn people to stone with a glance and to kill its opponents by breathing on them.

The two claws at the tips of its wings help the dragon grip onto trees.

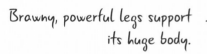

Brawny, powerful legs support its huge body.

This dragon has a large, rooster-like crest on its head.

The Cockatrice has vitreous, cold-blooded eyes.

Its forked tongue is like a snake's.

Marsupial Dragon

Compared to other kinds of dragons, the marsupial is relatively small. To make up for this reduced size, it has developed incredible stamina and agility. It has a mantle of greenish-brown scales, can breathe fire but looks very like a kangaroo, with the same ability to carry its young in its pouch. It also fights with its front legs like a boxer. Don't be misled into thinking it's a sweet little creature, though, bouncing across the Australian outback. It's still a powerful, wild animal.

The young dragon stays in its mother's pouch until it outgrows it.

It can stand on its hind legs, leaving the front ones free to fight opponents.

The scales covering this dragon are every color in the rainbow.

Rainbow Serpent

Although it might look to all intents and purposes like a snake, the rainbow serpent is a mythological creature with supernatural powers. It is linked to the creation of rivers, mountains, canyons and other parts of the Australian landscape. It makes the land fertile and restores aquifers. But don't think of the rainbow serpent as a gentle pet guardian. While it is kind to the people living and working the land it guards, it will also mercilessly punish anyone damaging it.

The rainbow serpent is featured in the Dreamtime stories of the Australian aborigines.

Dragon Training

Having completed the first part of this dragonology book, you'll now be able to recognize all the different types of dragon. The next step in your progression towards being a dragon trainer —which requires expertise and conviction— or a ruthless hunter of cruel dragons, is to understand a dragon's habits, behavior and needs. So, it's going to take a lot more than guts. Are you ready to start your training?

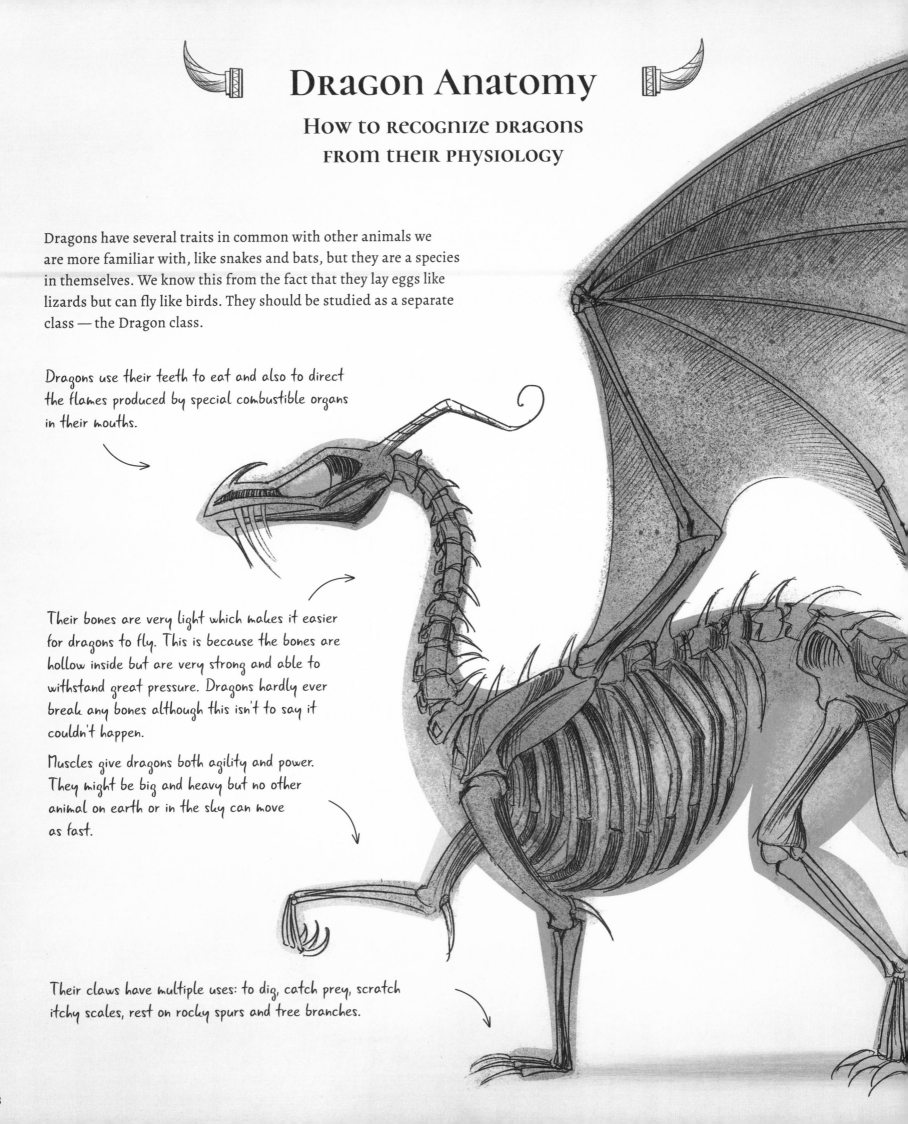

Dragon Anatomy

How to recognize dragons from their physiology

Dragons have several traits in common with other animals we are more familiar with, like snakes and bats, but they are a species in themselves. We know this from the fact that they lay eggs like lizards but can fly like birds. They should be studied as a separate class — the Dragon class.

Dragons use their teeth to eat and also to direct the flames produced by special combustible organs in their mouths.

Their bones are very light which makes it easier for dragons to fly. This is because the bones are hollow inside but are very strong and able to withstand great pressure. Dragons hardly ever break any bones although this isn't to say it couldn't happen.

Muscles give dragons both agility and power. They might be big and heavy but no other animal on earth or in the sky can move as fast.

Their claws have multiple uses: to dig, catch prey, scratch itchy scales, rest on rocky spurs and tree branches.

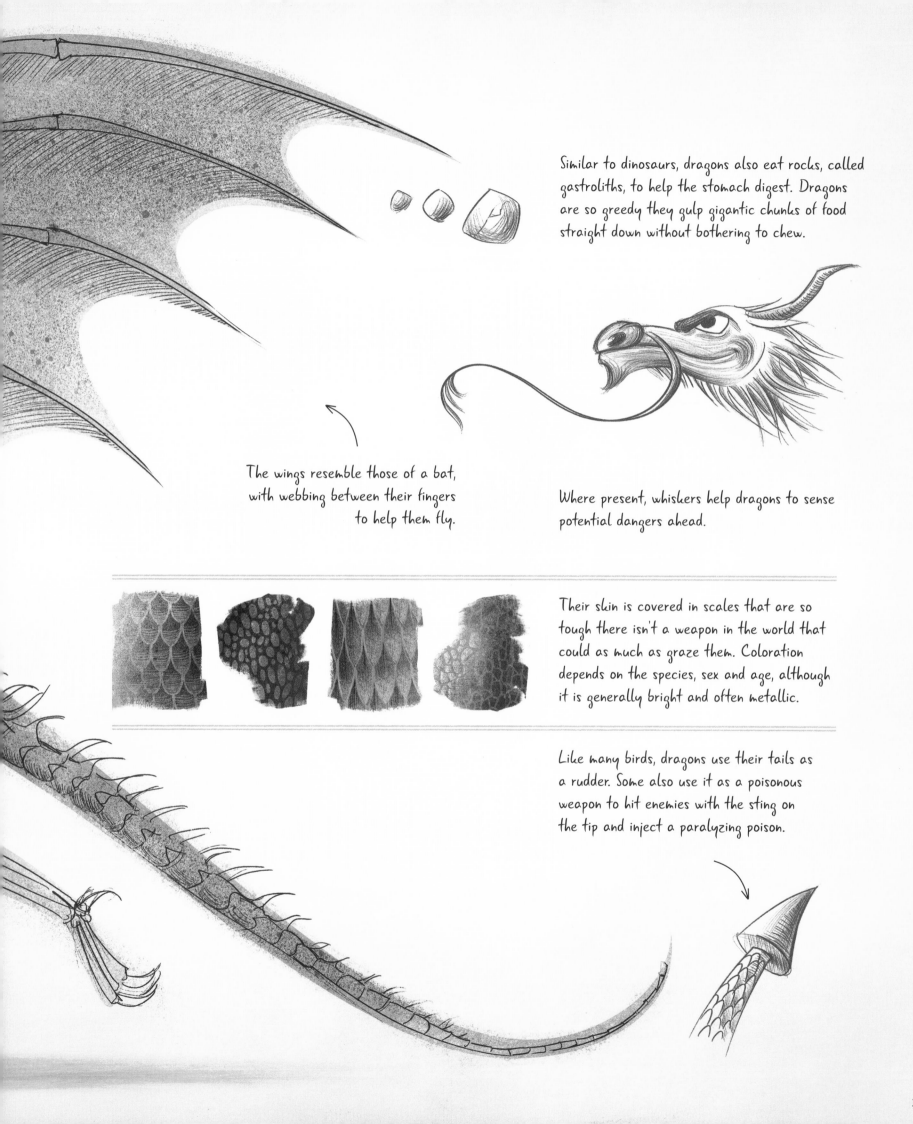

Similar to dinosaurs, dragons also eat rocks, called gastroliths, to help the stomach digest. Dragons are so greedy they gulp gigantic chunks of food straight down without bothering to chew.

The wings resemble those of a bat, with webbing between their fingers to help them fly.

Where present, whiskers help dragons to sense potential dangers ahead.

Their skin is covered in scales that are so tough there isn't a weapon in the world that could as much as graze them. Coloration depends on the species, sex and age, although it is generally bright and often metallic.

Like many birds, dragons use their tails as a rudder. Some also use it as a poisonous weapon to hit enemies with the sting on the tip and inject a paralyzing poison.

From Egg to Dragon

Everything you need to know to tackle the developmental phases of your dragon's life

Dragons live a lot longer than humans which is why their development is a lot slower. It takes several years, as many as three, for an egg to hatch, and many more after that for the baby dragon to grow, and yet more still for it to finally become an adult.

An Egg for all Tastes

There is no set size for dragon eggs. There are "tiny" ones that are a little smaller than an ostrich egg, and enormous ones that are as big as a baby hippopotamus. The coloration also varies from species to species, and depending on the color of the embryo growing inside the egg. Generally speaking, the eggs are fairly hard, and the dragon has to break them with a special horn which falls off afterwards. If you ever find an abandoned egg, keep it warm to help it hatch.

Some male dragons do up to ten loop-the-loops to win over a female!

Mommy and Daddy's Little Darling

Female dragons don't settle for the first male to come their way. They choose the ones which distinguish themselves for their more elaborate flying skills. But once a female has chosen her companion, it's for life. To begin with, the couple build a warm, comfortable den where the female can lay her eggs, usually three to five. It takes years for the eggs to hatch but to mom and dad's joy, their patience will eventually be rewarded when they see the muzzle of their babies finally pop out.

Naughty Pups

Just like human children, baby dragons are lively, noisy and restless. They also tend to get into trouble and have to be watched constantly because they climb up everything, even long before they've learned to fly. Likewise, there's also a chance of them setting things on fire until they learn how to control the flames they produce. It's always a good idea to keep a fire extinguisher on hand while they're getting the hang of it.

Dragons learn to fly on their own although they need time to learn the different techniques. In the early stages, it's a good idea to wrap them in something protective to make sure they don't hurt themselves when they fall.

Managing a Teenage Dragon

The most delicate stage in a dragon's development is when it is no longer a baby that can get away with anything but not yet a responsible adult. You'll have to be endlessly patient in this period because your dragon will get angry for the slightest thing, escape your control time and time again, demand its own way and undoubtedly get into all sorts of trouble, big and small. If you reward it with something tasty, like an extra steak, when it does something good, you'll make far more progress. And if your dragon happens to shut itself away in its cave with a big "Do not disturb!" sign outside, don't put its bad temper to the test. Just wait for it to come out by itself, even if it takes years!

It's all in the Training

Taming a dragon to live in the human world

Dragons are wild creatures, used to roaming free in their natural habitat, with coarse, often violent, ways. Even the calmest, most peaceful species can exhibit "uncivil" behaviors at times. It's crucial, therefore, that they get some training to stop them from causing any problems.

Good Table Manners

You can't expect your dragon to take its meals at the table, wipe its muzzle with a napkin, or eat with a knife and fork, but you can definitely train it not to dive at its food, gobble it down in a second and dirty everything around it. From a very young age, you must teach it to remain seated until dinner is served, to chew slowly and wipe its face after it's finished. To stop food from going everywhere, chop it up and put the chunks into a huge bowl.

The Rules of the Sky

The sky might not be quite as busy as the roads but anyone flying in it must learn to follow a number of rules, including right of way and speed limits. Your dragon will probably think it can do whatever it wants and you'll have to explain that, if it wants to stay safe, this is not a good idea. What would happen if it were to bump into a plane?! Dragons are intelligent creatures so if you give them a diagram, they'll soon pick up how to behave appropriately.

They can be very noisy eaters, at times, even risking setting fire to the forest. Explain to your dragon that it would be better to eat in a cave, where it's fiery breath won't be able to ignite any plants or trees.

The Rules of a Good Dragon

Make sure you hang the following list of
rules somewhere your dragon can see them,
say above its bed!

1.
No spreading stinks in public!

2.
No screaming, unless addressing someone
on the other side of a canyon!

3.
Think before getting into footfights!

4.
No snarling, unless it's to scare away an enemy.

5.
Only resort to fighting in the event of extreme
danger for yourself or your owner.

All dragons tend to put their fingers
up their nose. Teach them to blow
their nose on a large leaf.

Dragon Food

What to feed a dragon to keep it healthy

As you can probably imagine, dragons eat a lot. Some are easy to please and will accept anything, others have specific preferences and are harder to cook for.

When your dragon is digesting, don't stand too close. The flames that come out when it burps are terrifying!

Most dragons are carniverous so they're not very keen on vegetables but, whether they like it or not, they have to eat them! They'll be easier to convince if you serve the vegetables in a boiling-hot soup!

Never hide under a dragon's tail: if it suddenly needs to pee, you'll get soaked!

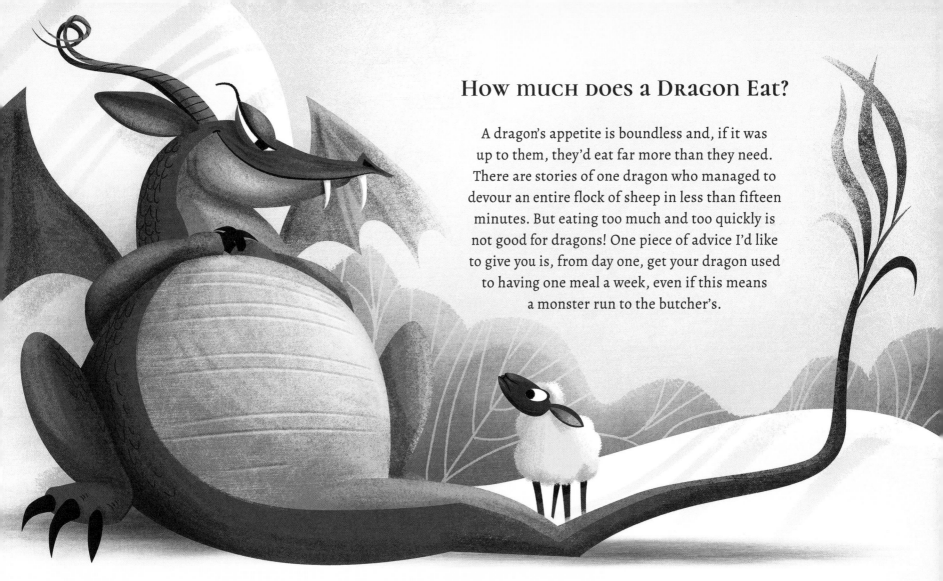

How much does a Dragon Eat?

A dragon's appetite is boundless and, if it was up to them, they'd eat far more than they need. There are stories of one dragon who managed to devour an entire flock of sheep in less than fifteen minutes. But eating too much and too quickly is not good for dragons! One piece of advice I'd like to give you is, from day one, get your dragon used to having one meal a week, even if this means a monster run to the butcher's.

Balanced Diet

A dragon's favourite food is definitely meat, red meat in particular, rare if possible. Some types of dragon also like fish, seafood first and foremost. Ice dragons have been known to accept squid, seals, and polar bears. Others have more specific tastes, like the anteater dragon with a penchant for termites, ants and any type of insect.

Waste Problems

Given how much they eat, try to imagine how much poop a dragon produces! What do to with it? Now that is a serious problem! If you can, try to teach your dragon to poop in a volcano. Otherwise, you'll need a sturdy shovel, a truck and time to get out to the countryside. Farmers say dragon poop is an excellent fertilizer so no doubt they'll take it off your hands.

Weaning Baby Dragons

Dragon pups are not like human babies: no milk for them! Their teeth are not very sharp, though, so while they're young, chop their food up carefully before spoonfeeding it to them.

Tricky Types

Dragons are known to be fiery, better tread carefully around them!

Some dragons are actually big softies, others can be grouchy; some are famous for their peaceful nature while others would pick a fight with the first person to go near them. In any case, the key thing to remember is that they are wild creatures, not pets.

Good Manners above all else

Here are some important ways to get off on the right foot with a dragon:

1.
Never look a dragon straight in the eye. Look down and try to be as least threatening as possible.

2.
Don't start to speak until the dragon gives you permission.

3.
Always use a friendly tone when speaking to a dragon.

4.
Be respectful and never underestimate the intelligence of the dragon before you.

Good or Bad-Tempered

Some species are naturally kinder than others, like the Chinese Lung for example, which is mostly friendly to humans, can be easily trained and is more likely to trust and be a friend to all those of pure soul approaching it. But this can vary a great deal from dragon to dragon. Among the Lungs, some can be temperamental, aggressive and not at all keen on conversation. They're all different, just like humans!

Developing Personalities

It's difficult to say, at birth, what kind of personality a dragon will have. Baby dragons are normally outgoing, noisy and extremely boisterous. If you get the chance to raise one from infancy, it will be easier to forge a strong bond with it. As they get older, dragons become more cantankerous. This is especially noticeable as they approach adulthood, the developmental stage we call adolescence, when they are impossible to handle. Weirdly, it's easier to reason with them as grown-ups than when they are young, adventure-seeking pups.

It's never a good sign when a dragon bellows smoke. Better take a step back and get out of the way of the flames, if you can.

The color of the scales changes on some dragons to reflect how they're feeling. Being able to recognize the different moods of the animal you're facing could come in very useful!

Between Sky and Sea

From ice to fire, dragons have adapted to every kind of habitat

Dragons feel most at ease when they're chasing prey in the air although they have no choice but to come down to land when it's time to eat. But don't think bumping into one will be easy. Dragons are very good at going under the radar!

Volcanoes are the Best!

Volcanic cones with smoking peaks, incandescent craters, spray from geysers, pools of boiling magma…Dragons love anything to do with ash and lava. The heat helps them to stay healthy, keeping their scales supple and adding even more fire-power to the flames they breathe. If you go looking for a dragon in a place like this, make sure you have the right equipment with you. At the top of your list should be a gas mask because volcanoes are usually surrounded by poisonous gases.

Be careful when a dragon emerges from a pool of boiling magma, it will shake itself like a wet dog after a bath!

Deep in the Forest

Some dragons that live in tropical areas with thick vegetation are very good at camouflaging themselves. You could very easily travel the length of a forest without ever spotting one, even though there may be a dozen around you. Forests are also the ideal habitat for wingless species slithering on the ground instead of flying in the sky. Like anacondas or other kinds of constrictor snake, they move along the ground or branches looking for animals to capture.

If you happen to be walking through a tropical forest, always check your back. You never know when you might have two dragon's eyes on you.

Ice Boots

Not all dragons love the heat. Some prefer parts of the world covered in ice and snow which they are able to walk on, thanks to the special pads on their feet. Their favorite place is the North Pole, also home to their favorite food - the polar bear. They won't sniff at the South Pole either, although penguins wouldn't be their first choice for lunch. At the end of the day, snow-capped peaks, wherever they are, offer only temporary refuge, as dragons prefer much bigger spaces!

Who do you think would win a head-to-head between a dragon and a yeti?

49

Deep in the Depths

Seas, lagoons or rivers anywhere dragons can dive into!

Many dragons will only go into the water to get rid of parasites and impurities. Others are experts are staying underwater and are just like regular sea creatures.

Storms and Whirlpools

Sea dragons are at their happiest when the sea is raging, the waves are white-capped and whipped up into giant vortices that suck everything down to the seabed. They love such extremes and the challenge they present. Skimming the waves with their webbed feet or dueling with the whirlpools gives them a chance to test their mettle and become even stronger in the process. Moreover, these are also the best places to catch other marine animals off guard, making them an easy catch.

Even dragons like to ride the waves in their own special way!

Muddy Waters

Dangerous creatures are also to be found in marshlands. Swamp dragons, for example, are a lot like crocodiles. They leave only their nostrils above the water to breathe and use their legs like oars to paddle through the reeds and water lilies, perfectly camouflaged in the greenish-brown water. They might not breathe fire like their land-dwelling counterparts but their attacks are just as deadly. They surprise their victims by injecting them with a killer poison.

Some people claim to have witnessed clashes between dragons and giant squid. Who do you think is the strongest of the two?

Sea dragons have developed a system that enables them to breathe underwater.

Squid Style

Some sea monsters have multiple heads and use a hunting system similar to that of the giant squid. Their hydrodynamic bodies enable them to slip through the water and sneak silently up on their prey before they grab and crush it in their long tentacles. A group of dragonsonce mistook a tanker for a whale. They grabbed it but immediately let it go when they realized it wasn't edible.

Luminous Dragons

Some dragons use methods similar to those of other deep-sea dwellers. One of these is bioluminescence, namely the ability to emit light and illuminate the dark depths. When they're under water, they emit a range of bright colors, like highlighter pens, making them look both surprising and terrifying at the same time.

Keeping your Dragon in Good Shape

How to stop your dragon from getting sick and to get well quick

It probably won't come as a surprise to learn that there are no medicines for dragons.
So you'll need to make sure your dragon never gets sick. But in case it does, you'll have
to summon all your courage, and also the necessary protective gear, and take care
of it just like you would any other pet.

Dragon Flu

Dragons love making their dens in rocks or underground caves, places
where there are also drafts galore. So despite being hardy animals they
can sometimes catch cold and end up with some very noisy coughs
and sneezes! Smelly dragon snot is not the worst of your problems,
though, as the unexpected jets of fire are far more worrying. At the
first signs of a cold, get your dragon into isolation to stop it from
spreading its germs, keep it warm, put lots of compresses on its
chest, volcanic mud if possible, and keep it well hydrated.

First Aid for Dragons

Emergency landings or collisions with other flying creatures can sometimes see your dragon end up with sprains, broken bones and other kinds of injury. Wings and legs are the most easily injured but it's not unusual to see gashes between scales, even though their skin is usually pretty tough. The first thing to do is clean the wound thoroughly to prevent infection. But be careful, don't use hydrogen peroxide or any other human remedies, just gallons of clean water!

Full Tummy

When dragons are hungry, they don't hold back and are wont to swallow anything, including things which can give them serious indigestion. One way to avoid this is to make sure your dragon eats a healthy, balanced diet. But if you'd rather let your dragon go hunting for its own food, as a way of staying fit and true to its dragon nature, watch out for the tell-tale signs of indigestion and take cover! Put plenty of leaves and moss over your dragon's tummy— you'll need a lot of it! — and brew an *Artemisia dracunculus* herbal tea, the perfect drink for healthy dragons.

Dragon Riding

Funny, adventurous and loyal: the best pet you could ever wish for

It's not easy to look after a dragon but the thrill and excitement that comes with it will make it more than worth it. Not just because there's a heart of gold beating behind its ough scales, but because there's also a playful soul behind the scary exterior.

Just like dogs, dragons love playing fetch! You can throw any one of these creatures a ball or a stick for hours on end, and they'll never tire of bringing it back to you.

Dragon Games

Many of the games that children of all ages play around the world are also firm favorites with dragons. Want to hear some?

- Hide and seek, but only in places where there are large enough objects for the dragons to hide behind;
- Cops and robbers, provided you can find enough dragons to make evenly-weighted teams;
- Water fights, if you can convince the dragons that the water balloons don't have to be as big as a house!
- Tug-of-war, even though you have very little chance of winning.

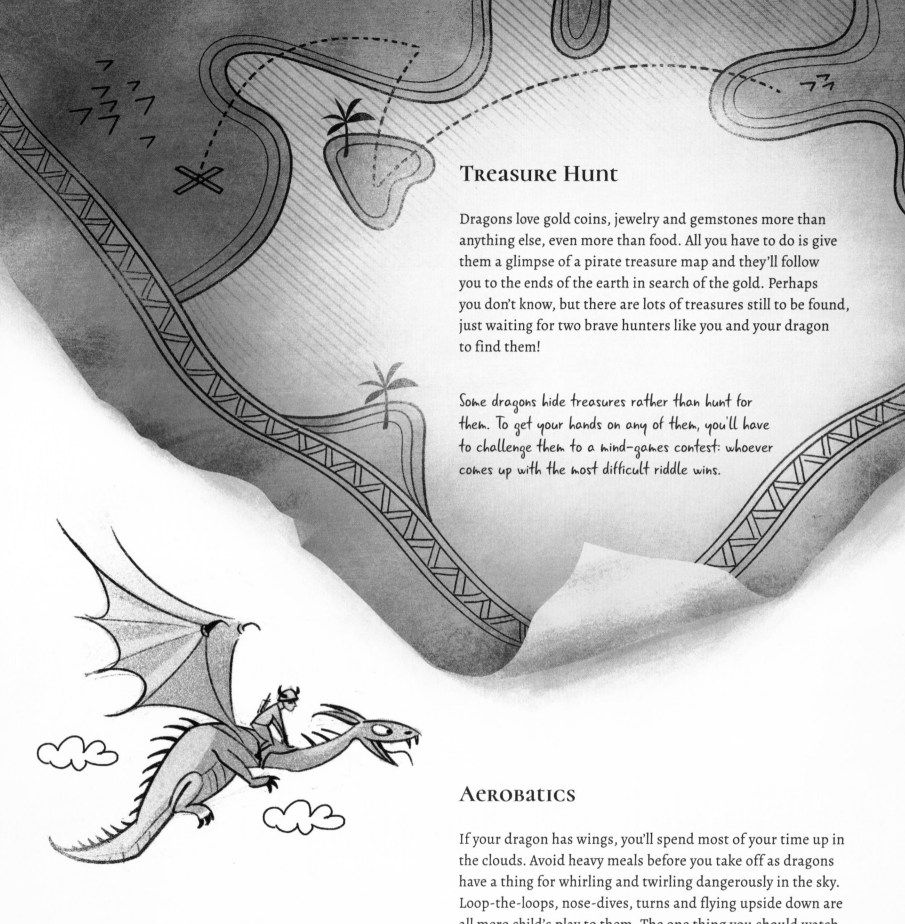

Treasure Hunt

Dragons love gold coins, jewelry and gemstones more than anything else, even more than food. All you have to do is give them a glimpse of a pirate treasure map and they'll follow you to the ends of the earth in search of the gold. Perhaps you don't know, but there are lots of treasures still to be found, just waiting for two brave hunters like you and your dragon to find them!

Some dragons hide treasures rather than hunt for them. To get your hands on any of them, you'll have to challenge them to a mind-games contest: whoever comes up with the most difficult riddle wins.

Aerobatics

If your dragon has wings, you'll spend most of your time up in the clouds. Avoid heavy meals before you take off as dragons have a thing for whirling and twirling dangerously in the sky. Loop-the-loops, nose-dives, turns and flying upside down are all mere child's play to them. The one thing you should watch out for are stalls. Some dragons like to stop suddenly mid-air and let themselves freefall. Something about the rush it gives them. If this should happen, don't be afraid as they'll start beating their wings again before you hit the ground. Just make sure you're holding on tight.

If you become an expert aerobatic dragon pilot you could be invited to take part in air shows alongside the world's most famous aerobatic teams.

Dragon-Riding

Riding a dragon is an art,
the art of falling off and getting back on again

Just like one lesson is not enough to become a competent horse rider, to ride a dragon
takes a long, long time, a lot of practice, incredible patience and the determination
to get back on every time you fall off.

Winning a Dragon's Favor

To ride a dragon you must first win its favor. If it doesn't
accept you, you'll never manage to get on its back. During
your first few lessons, your teacher will show you how to
establish a bond with your dragon. If you decide to teach
yourself, then try to tune into the creature's expressions
and gestures. If it nods or nudges you with its muzzle then
sniffs you, that's a good sign. If it backs away, or worse
still, bares its teeth, you're not doing so well!

Clothing and Protection

Before you climb onto your dragon, you need to first make
sure you have all the equipment required to respect rule 1,
also known as "flight safety", in the *Dragon-Riding
for Beginners Handbook*:
• Kevlar-lined helmet with fire-resistant visor
• Padded suit made of flameproof fabric
• Boots with metal spurs
• Parachute in case of mid-air unsaddling.

Saddle Baptism

Your first time in the saddle riding a dragon is something you'll never forget, especially because of the enormous bruises you'll have on your legs and bottom. Even if you manage not to fall off, sitting on the hard scales on the dragons' back for hours on end is anything but pleasant for the human skin. But in return for a few aches and pains, you'll experience something unique, a sense of freedom and power that you'll never get riding any other animal.

A saddle is the only riding accessory a dragon will let you put on it and, as you can well imagine, it needs to be extra big with handles to hang onto while you're riding.

Before you take off, you must learn the "Dragon Rules of Flight" by heart and pass a multiple choice test to be corrected by your personal dragon.

There is a flight hierarchy based on the importance of a dragon: the higher-ranking ones always have right of way!

Faster, Faster!

Dragons hate reins so don't bother trying to fit them. And they won't tolerate being hit with a riding crop either, so don't even think about trying to goad your dragon with one. What will work is the connection between the two of you. It will take time and some people say it's something only dragons can switch on when they decide the time is right. If you do manage to establish this psychic bond, rest assured your dragon will respond to your every command, so quickly you won't even have to time to give it.

It might be a good idea to put blinders on either side of the face of more jumpy dragons to keep them calm when in flight.

Dragon-Catching School

The art of flushing out, hunting down and defeating monsters

Strength alone is not enough to beat a dragon. You also have to be quick-witted, have a healthy dose of cunning, brains, intuition and, why not, plain good luck. Oh, and to be a professional dragon catcher, you also have to be very, very calm!

Brains First

Some impartial advice: never go into battle if you can avoid it. No matter how strong, well-trained and armed you are, a dragon will always be one step ahead. Better to have a good game plan, drawn up well in advance before you ever meet the monster.

When clashing with a dragon, it might be so impressed by your skills that it decides to stop fighting and become your friend.

Some dragons don't like their feet being tickled. Then again, it's not easy to get a dragon to lift its foot!

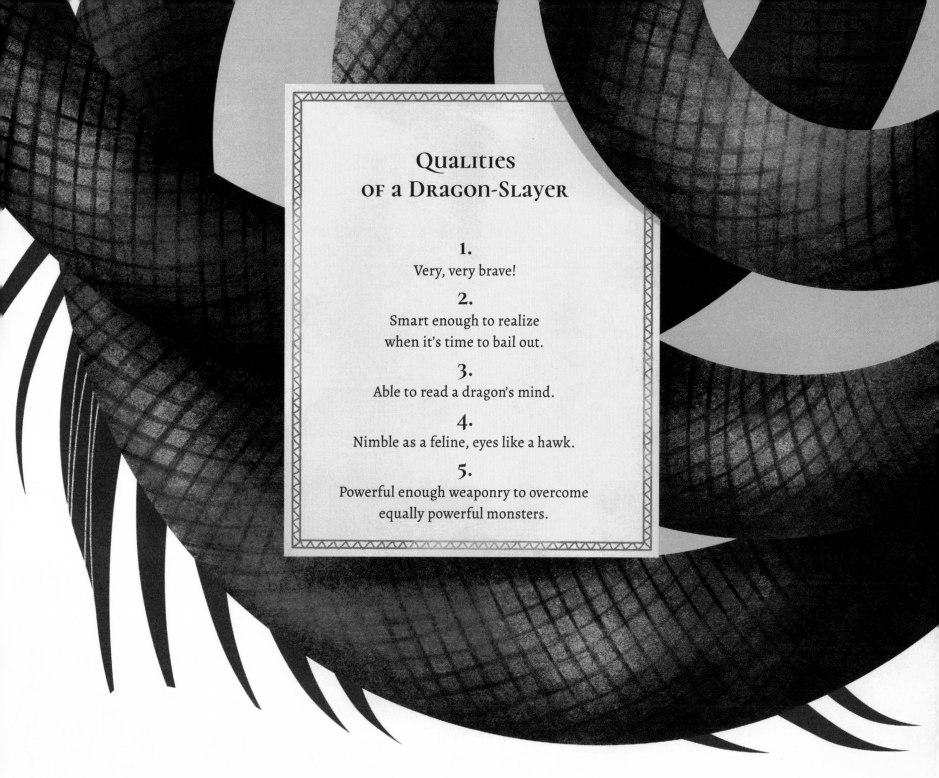

Qualities of a Dragon-Slayer

1.
Very, very brave!

2.
Smart enough to realize
when it's time to bail out.

3.
Able to read a dragon's mind.

4.
Nimble as a feline, eyes like a hawk.

5.
Powerful enough weaponry to overcome
equally powerful monsters.

Mind Games

Dragons are intelligent creatures and they know it.
This tends to make them rather vain and causes them
to lower their guard. If you learn now to use this hubris
against them, you could achieve much more than with
a sword. Showering them with compliments is
another way to gain their trust, win extra time,
study their behavior and work out how to defeat them.
If you're particularly talented, you could challenge
them on their own turf to a riddle contest,
relying on your wits to see you through.

Weaponry: Attack and Defense

If wits alone are not enough to outsmart a dragon
then you'll have to resort to weaponry, but with a few
precautions. Don't even think about using firearms — the
bullets will only bounce off their hard scales! You'll find
sharp weapons like spears and swords much more useful,
although you'll still have to try and wedge them between
the dragon's protective armor which, I can assure you, is
not easy! Safety gear will be absolutely essential: full body,
flame-proof, fire-resistant body armor and a giant shield
to protect you from the fire and blows.

Dragon Hunters

Famous legends about
dragon-slaying heroes

Not all dragons can be tamed. If anything, some are so dangerous they need to be eliminated to allow a village, a city or an entire nation to live in safety. To slay a dragon, though, clearly requires skills of a superhuman nature.

A Helping Hand

When you're trying to slay a dragon with multiple heads, like Heracles was, it's hard to do it by yourself. No matter how strong he was or how hard he tried, every time he chopped a head off, another two grew back. His nephew stepped in to lend a helping hand, searing the injured neck where Heracles had just cut a head off. It was an ingenious idea. Safety in numbers, they say, better not forget it!

Not surprisingly, Heracles killed a dragon. When he was still a child, he crushed two serpents with his bare hands!

The monster that Heracles killed lived in a terrible place: the swamp of Lerna. No wonder it was always angry!

TRICKS AND PLOYS

Sometimes artifice is an effective way to beat a dragon. This is what happened with the terrible, eight-headed Yamata no Orochi. After devouring seven young sisters, the beast threatened to eat the last remaining one, too. Susanoo, god of storms, arrived and had a special banquet laid out — eight vats full of sake — for the dragon's return. When Yamata no Orochi appeared, it went straight for the sake and drank every last drop of the alcoholic drink. It got so drunk it didn't realize it was about to die.

The legend of Yamata no Orochi ends in a marriage: between the god Susanoo and the beautiful young girl whose life was threatened by the dragon. Love always wins!

Saintly Intervention

There was once a terrifying dragon that lived by a spring in Cappadocia. To get close to it, the local people had to offer food, either animal or human sacrifices. This went on for many years until a brave young warrior called George arrived and, without giving it a second thought, vowed to take on the dragon. He didn't kill it, only made it as meek as a dog on a leash. George's actions were considered so exceptional he was made a saint.

Artifice, Courage and Strength

Some dragons are so tough they require multiple skills, both physical and mental, to overcome them. Sigurd, who was desperate to get his hands on the dragon Fafnir's gold, did exactly this. Renowned for his great strength but aware he couldn't defeat the dragon with strength alone, he dug a deep pit and lay in it waiting for the dragon to pass. When Fafnir was above him, Sigurd stabbed him with the legendary Gram sword.

When Sigurd got the blood of Fafnir on his hands, he gained the ability to understand any language.

Anna Láng

Anna Láng is a Hungarian graphic designer and illustrator who is currently living
and working in Sardinia. After attending the Hungarian University of Fine Arts in
Budapest, she graduated as a graphic designer in 2011. She worked for three years
with an advertising agency, at the same time working with the National Theatre
of Budapest. In 2013 she won the award of the city of Békéscsaba at the Hungarian
Biennale of Graphic Design with her Shakespeare Poster series. At present she is
working passionately on illustrations for children's books. In recent years she has
brilliantly illustrated a number of titles for White Star Kids.

Federica Magrin

Born in Varese in 1978, Federica has worked in publishing for more than ten years,
first as an editor at Edizioni De Agostini and currently freelancing. She tends
to focus on children's books but also writes educational texts and stories, and
translates novels. Over the years, she has done several books for White Star Kids.

WSkids
WHITE STAR KIDS

White Star Kids® is a registered trademark property of White Star s.r.l.

© 2019 White Star s.r.l.
Piazzale Luigi Cadorna, 6
20123 Milan, Italy
www.whitestar.it

Translation: Denise Muir

ISBN 978-88-544-1550-8
1 2 3 4 5 6   23 22 21 20 19

Printed in Italy by Rotolito S.p.A. - Seggiano di Pioltello (Milan)